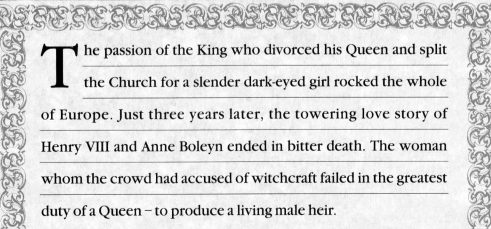

The passion of the King who divorced his Queen and split the Church for a slender dark-eyed girl rocked the whole of Europe. Just three years later, the towering love story of Henry VIII and Anne Boleyn ended in bitter death. The woman whom the crowd had accused of witchcraft failed in the greatest duty of a Queen – to produce a living male heir.

SECOND IN LINE

WHEN HENRY VIII WAS BORN IN THE SUMMER OF 1491, NO-ONE EXPECTED HIM TO BE KING. HE WAS THE SECOND SON, AND HIS ELDER BROTHER ARTHUR, BY THEN A STURDY LAD OF ALMOST FIVE, SEEMED SET TO SUCCEED TO THE THRONE

PRINCE HENRY CAME INTO THE WORLD ON 28 June in a rambling red-brick palace on the Thames at Greenwich, just across the river from the walled city of London. He was baptized just a few days later and called simply after his father. Henry VII was the first Tudor king, whose reign brought to an end the bloody Wars of the Roses. Prince Henry's young mother, the beautiful Elizabeth of York, went on to have four more children, but only one, the Princess Mary, survived infancy, and the Queen herself died in childbirth in her thirties.

Shortly after his third birthday Henry was created Duke of York, and the monarch's second son has been given this title ever since. His childhood, which he spent with his brothers and sisters at Greenwich and at other royal palaces and houses near London, was dominated by the frugal regime ordained by his strict father, a monarch who kept his children as firmly under his control as he did his newly won kingdom.

A strict childhood

Learning was the hallmark of a prince, and Henry was given an excellent education. With the famous poet and scholar John Skelton as his principal tutor, the young Duke was schooled in Latin, French, Greek, Spanish and Italian, learning to speak and write the first two fluently when he was still very young. He was also given a solid grounding in theology and it was not long before he showed a talent for music inherited from his mother, spending hours practising the lute and virginals.

On a typical day, Henry rose very early to attend six o'clock mass. His breakfast would be a cold meal of meat and bread washed down with ale or wine, and then he would spend the morning at his books. After dinner, which was much earlier than our lunch, the long afternoons were spent in sport and martial exercises, learning to shoot with the longbow, to ride in armour and to wield a huge two-handed sword.

Fine Art Society, London/Bridgeman

Music and other courtly pastimes were reserved for the evening, after the young Prince had heard evensong. Apart from Skelton, the other constant figure in the young Henry's life was his paternal grandmother, Margaret Beaufort, a severe and forceful matriarch who ruled the Royal nursery with a rod of iron.

The young Prince's first major public appearance was at the marriage of his elder brother Arthur to Catherine of Aragon in November 1501. Petite Catherine, the youngest daughter of Ferdinand and Isabella of Spain, had been solemnly betrothed to the Prince of Wales as early as 1489 and had long been preparing for

♔ *The new Tudor dynasty founded by Henry VII* left *was fated to last only three generations. Prince Henry, Duke of York* above, *was the only one of four sons to reach adulthood. He became the heir when his elder brother Arthur, Prince of Wales, died at 16 of tuberculosis*

Mary Evans Picture Library

the day when she would come to England. She was almost 16 and Arthur just 15 when they were thought old enough to marry.

Prince Arthur weds

Under the eyes of the gorgeously attired nobles and dignitaries filling the nave, Henry escorted the golden-haired bride up the aisle of old St Paul's Cathedral to the scarlet covered platform where Arthur awaited her, and led her out afterwards to meet the cheering crowds. For once, Henry VII was prepared to loosen the purse strings. The Duke of York was given a new suit of white velvet specially for the occasion and ten days of feasting and rejoicing followed, when all who saw Prince Henry noted his energetic and skilful dancing. A great tournament was held at Westminster to welcome the Spanish Princess, when thousands of spectators crowded the double-tiered stands around the tiltyard to see knights in full armour mounted on colourfully caparisoned horses run at each other with blunted lances.

But then tragedy struck. After less than five months of married life, the handsome, sensitive Prince of Wales died of the tuberculosis which had wasted his body for years. Henry VII and his

'Choose a wife for yourself; prize her always and uniquely'

HIS TUTOR'S ADVICE TO HENRY

Henry's mother, Elizabeth of York right, was vital to the new Royal line because of her Plantagenet blood. As the eldest child of Edward IV, her claim to the throne was actually far stronger than Henry VII's. Their marriage secured stability for the monarchy and peace for the country. Henry was born in the palace at Greenwich below. It became one of his favourite residences and it was there that he married Catherine of Aragon, Anne Boleyn and Anne of Cleves

National Portrait Gallery, London

Below This terracotta bust of a laughing boy is believed to be Henry VIII as a child. It dates from about 1500, when Henry was nine years old. His father had close contact with Italian courts and several Italian artists and sculptors came to England during his reign, bringing with them the new Renaissance style

By gracious permission of HM the Queen

👑 *Henry passed his childhood in the shadow of his sickly elder brother Arthur left who, as Prince of Wales, received the lion's share of their father's attention and was taught the difficult art of kingship from his earliest days. A strong family resemblance between the brothers is evident from portraits of the two as boys. Below A symbolic painting of Henry VII and his family. The King had seven children in all, only three of whom survived infancy. He is shown on the left with his three sons Arthur, Henry and Edmund while Margaret appears on the right with their four daughters Margaret, Elizabeth, Mary and Catherine. Edmund and Elizabeth died very young and Catherine only lived for a few hours. Over their heads, St George fights the dragon before the captive Princess Cleodolinde*

Both by gracious permission of HM the Queen

Queen were grief-stricken and, less than a year later, on her 38th birthday and ten days after the birth of a sickly daughter, Elizabeth of York was also dead. Now the young Prince Henry was the heir to the throne, his brother's pretty wife was a widow and his father a widower.

Deciding Catherine's fate

Dismayed at the thought of losing Catherine's dowry after he had spent so much on her wedding, Henry VII at first proposed to marry her himself, but Queen Isabella was deeply shocked by the idea, calling it 'a very evil thing'. King Henry was only 46, but he was ageing fast. His thinning hair was white, he was plagued by gout, and his few teeth were blackened stumps.

So Henry gave up any idea of marrying Catherine himself and instead betrothed her to his surviving son, in exchange for a second handsome dowry. The one difficulty was that both parties were God-fearing Catholics, and there is a text in the Bible which forbids a man to marry his brother's widow. Part of the Old

> '**H**aving already something of royalty in his demeanour in which there was certain dignity combined with singular courtesy'
>
> ERAMUS ON THE NINE-YEAR-OLD HENRY

4

Testament Book of Leviticus, it reads 'if a man shall take his brother's wife, it is an impurity; he hath uncovered his brother's nakedness; they shall be childless.' Catherine protested that the text did not apply because she and Arthur had never consummated their marriage, a claim backed up by the ferocious Spanish lady who was her constant companion. Most people thought Catherine spoke the truth, but the King could not afford any risk to the new Tudor dynasty and asked the Pope for a special dispensation to authorize the marriage.

The precocious Henry started to refer to his future wife as 'my dear and well-beloved consort, the princess my wife,' but his father, afraid of rumours which could lose him Catherine's much-needed dowry, would hardly let him see her and refused to set a date for the wedding until the dowry – a massive 100,000 scudos – had been paid. He guarded his son as carefully as if he were a girl, only allowing him out to take exercise if he was closely supervised and refusing him the least taste of independence. The Prince was terrified of his father, hardly daring to speak in his presence, and mumbling when the King spoke to him.

Long live Henry VIII

On 22 April 1509 the old King died, and Henry VIII exploded out of his years of repression. At only 17 years old, he was a physically superb young man and taking the wife who had been withheld from him for so long was of much greater importance than putting a few more gold pieces in his coffers. Casting aside his father's worries about the unpaid dowry, he married his Princess on 11 June at a private ceremony in the Chapel Royal at Greenwich. It was obvious to everyone that the couple were much in love. The age gap, which was later to become so significant, mattered not at all. He was almost 18, she was 23, and she had been waiting for her prince to come for almost ten years. A few weeks later, they were crowned in Westminster Abbey. The day before, cheering crowds had seen their new King dressed in scarlet velvet and a gold coat studded with diamonds, rubies and emeralds ride through streets draped in cloth-of-gold.

All England was delighted with him. Where Henry VII had been avaricious and miserly, his son was pleasure-loving and prodigal. And he was inordinately handsome. As a contemporary commented 'Nature could not have done more for him.' He was six foot two inches tall and perfectly proportioned, with broad shoulders, an athlete's body and a trim 32-inch waist. He had the fair skin that goes with red hair – and the proverbial redhead's temper. The thin, curiously high-pitched voice, the mean set to the lips and the small, piggy eyes – features which would become increasingly prominent as the years

THE MUSICAL KING

Henry VIII was one of England's most gifted kings and music was one of his greatest enthusiasms. He had a good singing voice and liked to accompany himself on the virginals or the lute, or to sing part-songs with his favourites among the court musicians. These men would be with him everywhere, and were among his closest personal servants. As well as playing, Henry liked to collect musical instruments. His collection included 26 lutes, as well as trumpets, viols, rebecs, sackbuts, fifes and drums, harpsichords and organs.

He invited some of the greatest performers of the day to England, among them the Dutch lute player Philip van Wilder and the celebrated Dionisio Memo, talented organist of St Mark's, Venice. Composers also found him to be a generous patron. Although there is no proof for the popular legend that Henry composed *Greensleeves*, he certainly wrote several pieces, including the songs *Pastime with good company* and *Helas Madam*; the religious motet *O Lord, the maker of all things*, and two masses for five voices, which would have been performed by the choirs of his Chapels Royal. He scoured England for these choristers and even stole singers from Wolsey's choir, of whose talent he was obviously jealous. An Italian visitor heard Henry's choir singing sacred music in the Renaissance style in 1516 and judged them to be 'more divine than human'. Henry seems to have been the last of the troubadour kings, a young man absorbed with dance and song, courtly love and the knightly virtues

British Library, London

♛Above *The score of Henry's song, 'Pastime with good company', one of several of his musical compositions which have survived to the present day. A beautifully coloured illumination* right *from Henry's Psalter depicts the King as a musician, playing the harp with his fool, Will Somers*

British Library, London/Bridgeman

University College, London

'This most
serene King
is...prudent and
sage, and free
from every vice'

THE VENETIAN AMBASSADOR
ON HENRY

*♛ Henry VIII and Catherine of
Aragon were crowned on 24 June
1509. This woodcut left is the
earliest contemporary printed
illustration of an English
coronation. Henry's Tudor rose is
carved above him, while Catherine
is identified by her badge of the
pomegranate*

passed – were outweighed by his height and
distinctive colouring. Vain of his appearance, he
was always magnificently dressed in sumptuous
silks, satins and velvets, and paid out vast sums
for the pearls and precious stones which
adorned his person and for the jewelled rings
which encrusted his fingers.

Earthy tastes were revealed in his
gargantuan appetite for food and drink and his
enthusiasm for the marriage bed. At this stage in
his life, Henry engaged in his sexual pleasures
with care. Most kings had mistresses, but if
Henry had love affairs at this time, he was careful
to be discreet. Promiscuity was not regarded as
lightly in the 16thcentury as it would be later and
adulterers were still regularly punished in the
church courts. Besides, Catherine was considered a beauty, as well as being cultured,

THE JOUST

The joust was one of the great spectacles of Tudor England. Knights encased in shining,
made-to-measure armour and mounted on massive warhorses thundered towards each
other on either side of a flimsy barrier, intent on unseating their opponents. The
horses were also armoured and carried a weight of some 450 pounds, while the
combined speed of the two contestants often reached 50 miles an hour. There would be
dancing and feasting and rich prizes for the winners. Even the poorest citizen could
enjoy the display, but such royal magnificence did not come cheaply. The 1511
tournament at Westminster, honouring the birth of his short-lived son, Prince Henry,
cost Henry VIII £4000, almost double the outlay on his 900-ton warship, the *Great
Elizabeth*. As Prince of Wales, Henry had shown great skill at jousting and when he
became King he could not resist taking part himself to show off his athletic prowess
but, as he aged, the risks increased. Once, in March 1524, he forgot to lower his visor.
The crowd shouted a warning but he thought they were cheering him on and dug his
spurs deeper into his horse, escaping serious injury only by a miracle. Several years
later he was violently thrown in a tournament at Greenwich, and was unconscious for
two hours. Like so many of Henry's pleasures, jousting was a young man's sport

birds on his great jewelled glove. Only very heavy rain kept him indoors and then he would be in a furious temper. On hunting and hawking days he would return just in time for supper at six o'clock – an enormous meal washed down with French red wine. A huge array of dishes would all be put on the table at once: great joints of meat side by side with elaborate sweets and bowls of fruit. Only after supper would he closet himself with his secretary to attend to State papers and diplomatic reports. The nobility encouraged him to enjoy himself, believing that a life of pleasure would stop him growing 'too hard upon his subjects as the King his father did'.

Yet Henry was no puppet monarch. He was an intellectually accomplished man as well: music was a consuming passion, and he was determined to be a great patron of literature and the arts. He even dictated theological books to his secretary, including *The Defence of the Seven Sacraments.*

But Henry's overriding aim in life was to father the male heir who would secure the Tudor line, and this was the goal which continually eluded him. In May 1510, Catherine had given birth to a stillborn girl. A year later, she had had an apparently healthy little boy, who was named after his father, but within weeks little Prince Henry was dead. Infant after infant was stillborn or lived only briefly, and Henry began to believe his marriage was cursed.

Windsor Castle, Royal Library © 1990 HM the Queen

intelligent and accomplished. The court was filled with attractive young women, but Henry had eyes only for his wife, wearing her colours on his sleeve when he jousted under the name of Sir Loyal Heart. To his subjects, Henry shone as a virtuous Christian king.

Hunting and hawking

An athletic young man, he gave full rein to his love of hunting, jousting, hawking, archery and every other kind of sport. Even cultivated and bookish gentlemen, like the poet Sir Thomas Wyatt, thought hunting and hawking were the basis of a good life in the country, with reading saved up for 'foul weather', but Henry turned hunting into a kind of endurance test, often tiring out eight or ten horses in a single day and riding 30 miles in pursuit of stags or a boar.

Every summer Henry took off for weeks at a time, turning the annual Royal progress through the southern half of England, which was the only opportunity for many subjects to see their king, into a hunting holiday.

If the ground was too frozen or wet for hunting, he went hawking, carrying the hooded

☙Above *Henry VIII in Parliament. Henry had strong ideas about the relationship between the Church and the Crown, which he was later to put into action, but at this time the Church still played a powerful role in government. The bishops and parliamentary abbots sit on Henry's right hand and the lay peers sit on his left. The judges sit in the centre on woolsacks and the clerks record the proceedings. The speaker of the House of Commons stands in the foreground facing the King.* Right *Catherine may seem plump and bland to modern eyes, but by the standards of her day she was quite a beauty. Creamy skin and a high, broad forehead set off her dark Spanish eyes. Plumpness was considered desirable and the Pope warned Henry before his marriage that Catherine should not undertake religious fasting without his permission, as it might harm her ability to bear children*

Kunsthistorisches Museum, Vienna

UNTOLD RICHES

Henry VIII, like many of his Tudor contemporaries, had a great passion for jewellery, and spent enormous sums of money on it. The Continent produced the most renowned master jewellers; many came to England to work for the King and members of his court. Hans of Antwerp was appointed the King's Goldsmith by Thomas Cromwell, 'Master of the King's Jewel House', and he, like other master goldsmiths, was supplied with designs by the great artists of the day, including Hans Holbein. Rubies were the favoured Tudor gemstone, followed in popularity by emeralds and sapphires

♔ Holbein's portrait of Henry *left* demonstrates the King's love of jewellery. The brim of his cap is trimmed with jewels in gold mounts alternating with triangular groups of pearls and gold cord. The black fabric of Henry's gown is decorated with gold cord trim in triple horizontal stripes, while the front and the tubular sleeves feature a pattern of gold braid 'gardes' crossed with golden clasps set with rubies. His 'false sleeves' of cloth-of-gold have as fastenings golden sleeve-clasps

🛇Henry is shown in full state in 1540 *right*. His semicircular mantle of cloth-of-gold is fully lined with ermine, and his jewel-trimmed black velvet cap surmounted by the Royal crown with two arches. Around his neck he wears a wide golden collar set with rubies and pearls and a gold chain from which a heavy jewelled medallion is suspended. On his left leg is the blue Garter; he received the Order when he was just three years old

🛇The windows of the Long Gallery of Hever Castle feature the coats of arms of the castle's owners. These include (from left to right in the photograph *left*) the joint armorial bearings of Henry and Anne Boleyn; Anne's coat of arms as Queen; Henry's coat of arms and that of Anne of Cleves. Before Anne Boleyn's marriage she was granted a coat of arms of six quarterings which alluded to her mother's descent, more illustrious than her father's, though both were descendants of Edward I. *Below* The arms of the Bullen (Boleyn) family are carved in stone over the fireplace in the Dining Hall of Hever Castle

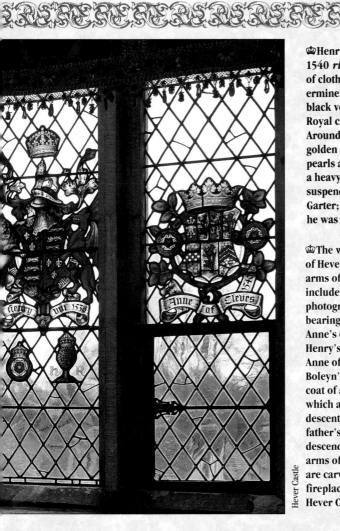

Hever Castle

Barber's Hall, London/Bridgeman

🛇A detail from a roll of parchment shows King Henry VIII processing to Parliament in 1512 *below*. In the procession are the Archbishop of Canterbury, the Duke of Buckingham carrying the Cap of Maintenance, and his son Lord Stafford carrying the Sword of State. Henry, wearing an ermine-trimmed blue velvet mantle and carrying a sceptre, walks under a canopy decorated with a Tudor rose. This red rose was the symbol of the unity of the houses of Lancaster and York, which came together to form the Tudor dynasty

Hever Castle

AN ELUSIVE ENCHANTRESS

EDUCATED IN THE FASHIONABLE FRENCH STYLE, ANNE BOLEYN RETURNED TO THE ENGLISH COURT IN 1522. HER FASCINATING WAYS ENCHANTED THE YOUNG MEN AND CAPTURED THE HEART OF HENRY

THE WOMAN WHO SWEPT HENRY OFF HIS feet was not especially beautiful. But she was sparkling, unconventional and very attractive to men. She was also exceptionally gifted and highly cultivated. And she came into Henry's life at just the right time.

Although she was distantly related to the King there was nothing about Anne Boleyn's early years to suggest that one day she might be Queen. Her family had moved to Kent at the end of the 15th century, and it was there, in the moated manor house of Hever Castle, that Anne may have been born about 1501. Her mother, Elizabeth Howard, was sister of the powerful third Duke of Norfolk. Her father, Sir Thomas Boleyn, was a soldier, courtier and diplomat.

But in the early years of his marriage, with only £50 a year to keep his family and household, Thomas Boleyn had to struggle to make ends meet. It was probably fortunate that, although Elizabeth bore him a child every year, only three survived. These were Anne, her brother George and her elder sister Mary.

Sir Thomas was extremely ambitious, for his children as well as himself, and particularly for his vivacious daughter Anne. In 1513 he packed the slim, dark-haired child of 12 off to Belgium, where the Archduchess Margaret of Austria, then Regent of the Netherlands, presided over one of the most sophisticated courts in northern Europe. There, Anne mixed with a glittering company of young courtly attendants.

Hever Castle

⚜ *Anne's father, Thomas Boleyn, quickly climbed the ranks of Henry VIII's court. A brass image of him remains at Hever Church above*

⚜ *Although her childhood was spent in the peaceful obscurity of Hever Castle, the Boleyn family home in Kent left, Anne soon made an appearance in the glittering European courts. She would later turn her quick wit and her unconventional dark beauty right to her advantage in the English court where the men found her fascinating*

A F Kersting

'*Most attractive*

of her features

were her eyes,

which she well

knew how to use'

A POET AT THE FRENCH COURT
ON ANNE

National Portrait Gallery, London

'Nature could not have done more for him.

He is much handsomer than any sovereign

in Christendom'

A CONTEMPORARY OF HENRY'S

CHILD PAWNS

In Tudor times, children of noble birth were not expected to marry for love, or to be able to choose their spouse for themselves. Royal children and the sons and daughters of the aristocracy were all treated as pawns. Married with care, they could be used to seal an alliance, revive family fortunes and generally solve their elders' problems. Neither Henry VIII nor Sir Thomas Boleyn would have thought twice about condemning their children to a loveless match provided the terms were right, and the fact that Catherine of Aragon and the young Henry VIII did fall very much in love was just a lucky accident. Royal children often found themselves condemned to share their bed with a consort whom they loathed, as when Henry's beautiful younger sister Mary was married to the ageing Louis XII of France. Their fate was often sealed when they were barely out of the cradle and not old enough to understand what was going on. Catherine of Aragon had originally been promised to Henry VIII's elder brother Arthur when she was two-and-a-half years old and her prospective husband not yet two

♛ Henry was about 30 years old and had not yet fallen under Anne's spell when this portrait was painted left. And while his wife Catherine was by this time showing signs of ageing, Henry was still a magnificent-looking man whose natural advantages were enhanced by sumptuous costumes of silk, satin and velvet

She learned the accomplishments of a fine lady, made music, listened to poetry, mixed with painters and sculptors and acquired the basis of her elegant French, which was the international language of court life.

Anne made an excellent impression in Malines, and her sophistication and poise did not go unnoticed when she returned to England in 1514. Although still very young, she was chosen to accompany Henry VIII's light-hearted and beautiful 18-year-old sister Mary to the French court, where Mary was to marry 53-year-old Louis XII of France.

In France, the prematurely senile Louis sent most of his wife's attendants away in a fit of jealousy. Anne was one of a handful of servants the tearful Queen was allowed to keep. Mary was soon back in England, however, freed from her ghastly new husband by his convenient death less than three months after the wedding. Anne accompanied her mistress home, but returned to France, together with her sister Mary, when their father was appointed ambassador to the French court in 1519.

A sea of indulgence

Things were now very different. Francis I, who succeeded Louis XII, was a witty, elegant and sensual 20 year old who presided over the most dissolute court in Europe. His courtiers were expected to have affairs, and the King would openly ask them the names of their mistresses and details of how they liked to make love. The Boleyn girls were attached to Queen Claude, Francis's square and dumpy wife, whose apartments provided an island of sobriety in this sea of indulgence. But they could not escape what was going on around them.

Warm-hearted Mary Boleyn soon became the mistress of the King and subsequently of one courtier after another. It was one thing to be the King's mistress, but quite another to be at everyone's disposal. She returned to England and was married off to William Carey.

Anne was a different proposition altogether. By the summer of 1520 she was 19. By the conventions of the time, which required women to be fair and golden-haired, Anne, with her olive skin and black hair, was not considered beautiful. She had a large black mole in her neck and a small deformity on her right hand, where a tiny second nail grew out of one of her fingers. But men found her fascinating. She was graceful and elegant and quick-witted.

Hever Castle

♛ *Not as clever or as sophisticated as her younger sister, Mary Boleyn left made the mistake of scattering her favours too widely and of being too open about her affairs within the French court. When Francis I referred to her as the most promiscuous lady at his court it was clear Mary had broken even the dissolute French court's code of behaviour. She soon found herself back in England where she was swiftly married off to one of Henry's young minions, William Carey. However, her marriage did not prevent her from having a discreet affair with Henry VIII*

Louve, Paris/Bridgeman

She could sing and dance well and perform on the clavichord and lute, and it was while in France that she probably put together a book of motets and French songs. Above all, she had the most expressive eyes, two deep black pools which seemed to promise everything and led her suitors on. But, although Anne became an expert flirt and loved to tantalize, she always kept her admirers at a distance.

By 1522, when impending war with France brought Anne back to England, her father had been appointed Controller of the King's Household, one of the most important positions at court in 1520. He also was now a rich man, his fortunes transformed by inherited estates. Anne was briefly betrothed to her distant Irish cousin James Butler, but she refused to have the young man when she saw him.

♛ *Above Francis I, the young French King, promoted romantic intrigues in his lascivious court. And it was said that the King himself 'slipped readily into the gardens of others and drank the waters of many fountains,' enjoying dozens of daughters, wives and mothers in addition to his many official mistresses*

Henry **VII** (1457-1509) m. *Elizabeth* (1465-1503)

Thomas Boleyn (d.1493) m. *Elizabeth* (d.1538)

Arthur (c.1487-1502) *Margaret* (1489-1541) *Mary*

Mary Boleyn (d.1543) *George Boleyn* (c.1504-1536)

Henry **VIII** (1491-1547) m.(1) *Catherine of Aragon* (1485-1536)

Mary **I** (1516-1558)

Elizabeth **I** (1533-1603) m.(2) *Anne Boleyn* (c.1501-1536)

m.(3) *Jane Seymour* (c.1509-1537)

Edward **VI** (1547-1553) m.(4) *Catherine Howard* (1521-1542)

m.(5) *Anne of Cleves* (1515-1557)

Brief Union m.(6) *Catherine Parr* (1512-1548)

FIELD OF THE CLOTH OF GOLD

In the scorching June heat of 1520 Henry VIII and Francis I, the young King of France, staged an event which became known as the eighth wonder of the world. Each monarch, accompanied by an entourage of some 5000 nobles and ladies, met in a valley on the border between France and Calais, England's last foothold on the Continent. Here, in a city of some 3000 silken tents, they jousted, feasted and made merry for three weeks. The Kings were both fine young men in the prime of life, Henry just a few days short of his 29th birthday and Francis 26, and they were determined to outdo each other.

Francis had a tent of gold brocade 60 feet round, its canvas roof studded with stars made from gilded foil. But this beautiful pavilion was overshadowed by the Italianate palace which Henry had built, its rooms bigger than any in the royal palaces of England and with fountains in the central courtyard spouting claret and beer. A chapel was filled with priceless statues and crucifixes, and the rooms were hung with cloth-of-gold so splendid that the valley became known as the Field of the Cloth of Gold. The English brought every tent peg, cushion and 3000 horses across the Channel, carried in a fleet of 27 ships.

Henry excelled in the jousting, tiring horse after horse but, when he challenged Francis to a wrestling match, the French King threw him to the ground, an indignity which no English courtier dared report.

Catherine of Aragon accompanied her husband, her long hair hanging free over her shoulders, and the ladies of the French party probably included the young Anne Boleyn, who must have watched the proceedings with amazement

⚓Below *Henry VIII's embarkation from Dover en route to the Continent took place on 31 May 1520. The King and his suite probably sailed aboard the* Henri Grace-de-Dieu, *the largest vessel in the Tudor navy, which was adorned with streamers and shields and powered by golden sails*

By gracious permission of HM the Queen

Soon after the strong-willed Anne made her court début in the company of her sister, she began to be noticed. The poet Sir Thomas Wyatt, still in his teens, was one of the many young men she enchanted, but he was already married. More serious was her involvement with Lord Henry Percy, son of the powerful Earl of Northumberland. Anne and Percy contrived to see each other every Sunday morning during the spring of 1522, when the young man was one of those who accompanied Cardinal Wolsey, the King's chief minister. But his romance with Anne was doomed. Someone informed the King of Anne and Percy's passionate tête-à-têtes. Henry flew into one of his terrifying rages and instructed Wolsey to separate the couple. Consciously or not, Henry was not prepared to see Anne in another man's arms.

Love turned cold

By now, Henry's once joyous marriage had turned sour. Catherine was still loyal and devoted but she was now approaching 40. She had still not produced an heir to the throne and, as each year passed, it became less and less likely she would ever do so. The Princess Mary, born at Greenwich on 18 February 1516, was the only one of Catherine's children to have survived.

A few years earlier Henry had had a long-lasting affair with Bessie Blount, one of Catherine's ladies-in-waiting, who in 1519 had given birth to his son, Lord Henry Fitzroy. Henry

♛ *Several of the events which took place at the Field of the Cloth of Gold were recorded by an unknown artist above. The elaborate English palace with its fountains flowing with wine and beer, especially created for the event, is seen in the right foreground. Henry's arrival at Guisnes is in the left foreground, while other sections of the painting depict various tournaments, banquets and groups of people*

'I beseech you now...to let me know your whole intention, as to the love between us two'

HENRY TO ANNE

also discreetly enjoyed the favours of Anne's sister Mary, even after she was married. The Queen turned a blind eye to these liaisons, secure in the expectation that Henry's ardour would soon cool and die.

But Anne was different. She was sufficiently intelligent and worldly-wise to see that the stakes were high. When Henry finally succumbed to her charms it is impossible to be sure, but it was probably in about 1526, when Anne was 25, that he fell desperately in love with her, his passion stoked and fired by her repeated refusals to sleep with him. For a hunter like Henry, her elusiveness added to the thrill of the chase. Anne flirted with him in the same light-hearted way that she teased other men, but used her dark eyes also on Sir Thomas Wyatt, who was now irrevocably separated from his wife.

Matters came to a head when she recklessly gave both men tokens of her affections, presenting Henry with a ring which he proudly displayed on his little finger, and Wyatt with a small jewelled tablet which he hung around his neck. The King, furiously jealous, seized his opportunity when the two men met over a game of bowls. When they disagreed about a cast, Henry deliberately pointed his ringed finger at the poet and insisted: 'Wyatt, I tell thee it is mine.' In answer, Sir Thomas pretended to measure the cast with the ribbon of the jewelled tablet. Henry's face turned black with fury and he strode away. Anne managed to smooth things

over, but she never repeated her mistake.

Henry's ardour grew month by month and, when Anne withdrew to her father's house to escape his constant attentions, he pursued her there with letters. For at least a year, she made him work hard. None of her replies have survived, but the tone of Henry's entreaties, in which his distress leaps off the page, suggests she was trying to discourage him. 'I must of necessity obtain this answer of you, having been above a whole year struck with the dart of love, and not yet sure whether I shall fail, or find a place in your heart and affection.'

Possessing Anne

Unable to restrain himself, he put the question to her directly. Was she prepared 'to do the duty of a true and loyal mistress, and give up yourself, body and heart, to me?' The pathetic final sentence, 'no more for fear of boring you', gives a glimpse into the state of mind of the man who had never before had to plead for anything.

Shortly after he wrote this letter Henry must have finally offered to marry her, because Anne declared she loved him with a love as rare as his and that she looked forward to sleeping with him after their marriage. Henry was jubilant.

At a ball given to honour the French ambassadors who had come to negotiate the marriage of his daughter Mary to the Dauphin or another French prince, the King astonished the assembly by leading out Anne as his partner. Their relationship was a secret no longer, and the King had set his mind on a divorce. Only through marriage could he finally have Anne and sire the heir which God had so far denied him.

♛ *Anne's involvement with Lord Henry Percy above, then heir to vast estates and numerous castles, could have led to a splendid marriage alliance. However, Percy had already been promised to another, and news of Anne's romance infuriated the King who soon had the couple separated*

White satin cuffs divided into eight panels and embroidered with floral patterns in coloured silk and golden thread

Soft buff-coloured leather gloves, with ruched rose-coloured silk edged with gold lace at the wrist

Tunic made of alternate stripes or 'plites' of damask (patterned cloth-of-silver) and plain gold, with a wide embroidered border

♛Henry at the Field of the Cloth of Gold in 1520 *left*. A contemporary chronicler recorded that 'his grace was apparelled in a garment of cloth of silver, of damask, ribbed with cloth of gold, so thick as might be; the garment was large and pleated very thick…of such shape and making that it was marvellous to behold'

♛Henry *below* wearing a flat-crowned hat, its edges tied with gold laces. His stomacher (a decorative panel worn over the chest and stomach) has gold-on-black embroidery and double rows of pearls; this is worn over a gathered shirt with an embroidered neckband

Long-sleeved rose velvet doublet with 'cuttes' or slashes on chest and sleeves

One sleeve is of silver damask lined with gold, the other of gold lined with silver

Thigh-high yellow leather boots with 'cuttes'

♛Every inch a king *right*. Henry's coat, of purple velvet, is a loose garment, narrower at the shoulders than at the hem, which is probably mid-calf in length. Strips of ermine trim the V-shaped collar, as well as the front opening and cuffs. Underneath he wears a doublet of cloth-of-gold with fur-trimmed, richly jewelled sleeves

Lynne Robinson

TUDOR SPLENDOUR

In an age of magnificence, Henry VIII was the most magnificent of beings – 'the best-dressed sovereign in the world: his robes are the richest and most superb that can be imagined'. He delighted in bright colours and exquisite jewels and, charmed by the dress of Francis I and his court, introduced many French fashions to England. Both men and women wore clothes of lush, colourful fabrics, slashed to show the material underneath, richly embroidered and, often, with precious stones sewn in

♛ *Right* Henry playing 'tenyse' or tennis, 'at which game it is the prettiest thing in the world to see him play, his fair skin glowing through a shert of the finest texture,' according to the Venetian ambassador at the time. After the game, so he wouldn't get a chill, he would wrap a tennis coat around himself – he had one of black velvet and another of blue

Henry used a triangular racquet; the cords were made of sheep's or goat's guts

A less expensive racquet which was a circle or square of wood with a long handle

Shirt of fine fabric with a square neck, gathered and delicately embroidered in 'Spanish work'

'Slops' or shorts of slashed silk or velvet, trimmed with gold cord

An example of 'Spanish work' – embroidery in black silk that was the most fashionable form of decoration for the necks and wrists of shirts and other garments

Henry's surcoat is a knee-length garment turned back at the neck to form revers. The sleeves are long and tubular, with the wearer's arm emerging from the vertical slit above the elbow

White shirt of fine fabric with frilled wrists. Because Henry's neck was thick and short, he always wore a small, turned-down collar

♛ *Left* Henry aged 51, wearing a deep blue silk doublet braided with silver and trimmed with rubies set in gold mounts at the front opening and sleeves. Over the doublet he wears a sleeveless garment known as a vest, which fastens at the waist and covers his back but not his chest. The pleated skirt is attached to the vest. His surcoat, of deep red velvet, is richly embroidered with gold and lined with sable

♛ *Above right* This 'nightgown' (actually a dressing-gown), a gift from Henry to Anne, is a long, loose, wrap-over garment of black satin lined with taffeta and trimmed with velvet. Over her hair she wears a 'bag-back hood'; that is, one with a bag-shaped back to hold her long hair

Two white silk scarves tied at the waist; a dagger and tassel hangs from one of these

♛ Anne wearing a 'French hood' of black velvet edged with pearls and trimmed with golden gauze *below*. Underneath, to secure the hood, she might have worn a cap similar to the one illustrated *below right*

Tudor doublets and surcoats often featured intricate interlaced embroidery patterns in gold. This example is from one of Henry's doublets, and shows the white shirt worn underneath puffing out through the 'cuttes' in the fabric

♛The costume *right* is typical of one worn by noblewomen in the 1540s. The gown, of cloth-of-silver, has very wide sleeves turned back to show the squirrel lining. The skirt is open at the front; underneath is a rose-pink silk underskirt with an embroidered border

Long jewelled girdle fastened at the narrow waist of the close-fitting bodice

Perfumes were fashionable among the wealthy, to disguise body odours (people rarely washed) and to ward off disease. The pomanders below contained balls of perfume and were hung from chains fastened to the waist

DIVORCE AT ANY PRICE

TORMENTED BY HIS DESIRE FOR ANNE AND HIS DESPERATION FOR A MALE HEIR, HENRY REALIZED THAT THERE WAS ONLY ONE WAY OUT

Cardinal Wolsey knew his position depended upon being able to procure a divorce, and he spent several months dreaming up strategies with the King left. Catherine below watched the manoeuvres with sorrow and disbelief

FOR HENRY TO DECIDE TO DIVORCE HIS AGEING Queen was one thing. Obtaining a divorce was quite another. Henry was a good Roman Catholic, attending Mass every day and religiously observing the Church's fasts, when no meat was eaten (although he made up for them on every other day, when he gorged himself with boar and venison). Furthermore, he was passionately interested in theology, and had even written a tract against the Protestant reformer Martin Luther, for which the Pope had awarded him the title of Defender of the Faith in 1521. The Church he had defended had married him to Catherine, and only the Church could sever their bonds.

Henry's winning card, as he thought, was the Papal dispensation which had allowed him to wed the wife of his elder brother. If this

had been taken and ransacked by the troops of the powerful Holy Roman Emperor Charles V, Catherine's nephew, who ruled over half of Europe. With Pope Clement now the Emperor's prisoner in the Vatican, he was hardly likely to give his blessing to a divorce which involved Charles's aunt. And Catherine herself found out what was going on and confronted Henry with what she had heard. There was an agonizing scene. Henry, stammering slightly through nerves and guilt, told her they had been living in mortal sin for 18 years and must part: his conscience could not allow him to be with her a moment longer. The Queen, in tears, stoutly maintained that their marriage was true, that she and Arthur had never made love and that she came to Henry's bed a virgin. Henry tried to calm her and the interview ended quietly, but watchful courtiers noticed that Henry was no longer on cordial terms with his wife.

♛ *According to tradition, Anne* below *used to sit at a bay window at Hever Castle to watch the King arrive* left. *But Henry was not a frequent visitor, and fear of contagion kept him away during the sweating epidemic; in fact, he fled to Waltham where the sickness had not yet arrived*

Mansell

Hever Castle

dispensation could be shown to be invalid, then the marriage had effectively never taken place. Henry's cunning and devious mind also came up with a second line of attack: even if there had been nothing irregular about the dispensation of 1503, it could still be invalid if the Pope had overstepped his powers in granting it. If the Bible were literally the word of God, then not even the Pope had the authority to go against what it said – and the text in the Book of Leviticus stated quite firmly that a man should not marry his brother's wife.

Divorce strategy

Henry and his chief minister, Cardinal Wolsey, worked out how the King could divorce Catherine without anyone being able to contest the case, and without her or anyone else knowing anything about it. Only a few days after the ball for the French ambassadors, Wolsey, who was also the Pope's representative in England, summoned Henry to appear before himself and the Archbishop of Canterbury, and charged the King with unlawfully cohabiting with his brother's wife for 18 years. But after a few sessions the proceedings were abandoned. Perhaps King and Cardinal realized they would never get away with what was really an elaborate farce, and decided the question of the divorce must be referred to Pope Clement VII.

Matters soon became very much more complicated. In June 1527, an exhausted, travel-stained messenger brought the news that Rome

It was soon common knowledge that Henry intended to dissolve his marriage. Everywhere tongues wagged and people murmured their disapproval. Catherine was popular, and for the King to strike out against her in order to marry a brazen upstart who was not even of Royal blood was almost beyond belief. People started to call Anne a 'goggle-eyed whore' and a 'six-fingered witch', and to murmur that she had cast a spell on the King. Anne was now at Hever again, and Henry, who was spending his summer hunting as usual, sent messenger after messenger galloping down to Kent with rich gifts and pleading letters. 'For myself the pain of absence already is too great,' he wrote, wistfully hoping that she might perhaps relent and become his lover before they were married. Anne seems to have blown hot and cold. But even if she did have second thoughts, perhaps sensing the streak of vicious cruelty in Henry's nature, there was no way out for her now. Too much was at stake. Charles V, deeply shocked to hear of the divorce proceedings against his aunt, had promised to help her in any way he could. What had started as a private affair was rapidly turning into a major international incident.

Undeterred, Henry sent a stream of agents

> ## 'I would you were in my arms, or I in yours; for I think it long since I kissed you'
>
> HENRY TO ANNE

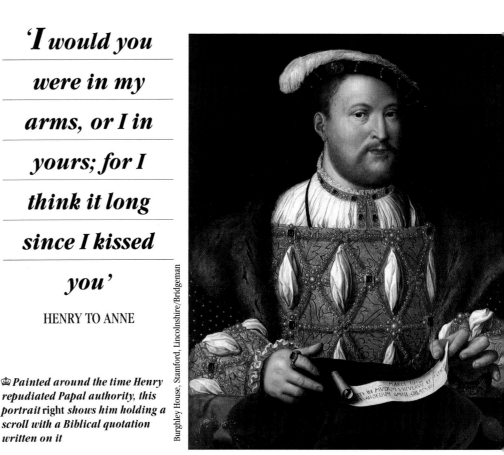

Burghley House, Stamford, Lincolnshire/Bridgeman

👑 *Painted around the time Henry repudiated Papal authority, this portrait* right *shows him holding a scroll with a Biblical quotation written on it*

post-haste across Europe to pester the Pope with his case. Eventually, in the summer of 1528, worn down by the constant badgering, Clement agreed that the case could be tried in England. The judges were to be Wolsey and a fellow cardinal from Italy, the worldly-wise Campeggio.

A threatening epidemic

The spring was warm that year, the palace gardens were full of flowers and the woods cool and inviting. For Henry and Anne, strolling beneath the trees and enjoying long picnics in the open, life must have seemed very sweet. But then came terrifying reports from upriver. The deadly sweating sickness, which had first swept across England in 1485, was killing people at a phenomenal rate. The sweat arrived in London on 14 June 1528. Anne was struck down, and carried swathed in blankets to Hever, where she nearly died. Henry sent his physician, Dr Butts, to care for her and wrote to her anxiously. Perhaps because of this narrow escape, or because Cardinal Campeggio had finally arrived from Rome to try the King's case, the lovers seemed to draw closer together. Unspoken desire flowered between them, erotic and unmistakable, and Henry began to caress Anne openly. As the French Ambassador reported to Francis I, 'the King is so infatuated, that none but God can cure him'. In the summer, Henry had written to Anne passionately, 'wishing myself (especially of an evening) in my sweetheart's arms, whose pretty breasts I trust shortly to kiss'.

WITCHCRAFT

Mary Evans Picture Library

Rumours about Anne Boleyn's supposed witchcraft had begun to circulate even before her Coronation. The break with Rome had been widely unpopular, and many people blamed Anne for what they saw as an ungodly act inspired by the Devil. And when Anne began to suffer repeated miscarriages it appeared that their suspicions were confirmed, since it was a common belief that witches gave birth to deformed creatures and stillborn children. According to popular legend, Anne called her pet wolfhound Urian, a name ascribed to one of Satan's followers, and she bore two marks associated with witches – a mole on her neck and a slight deformity of one of her hands. Certainly, when he began to tire of her, Henry found it easiest to ascribe his former obsession to sorcery. Witches were thought to be capable of seducing men through their kisses, and the detailed description presented at her trial of the way in which Anne had kissed her suitors fitted in with the theory that she had lured them to bed by her supernatural powers

Harrogate Museums and Art Gallery/Bridgeman

👑 *At the divorce hearing in 1529 Catherine refused to climb down, and pleaded with Wolsey and Campeggio to refer the case to Rome* above. *The Pope never approved the divorce, and issued a bull against it in 1533* left, *which Henry chose to ignore. In the meantime, Catherine refused to abandon the title of Queen*

'But alas! farewell to my time and youth spent to no purpose'

ANNE

MENAGE A TROIS

All this time, Henry was living under the same roof as both his wife and sweetheart. Despite his threat to send her away, Catherine remained at court. Her composure recovered, she carried on as if nothing had happened, and treated Anne with exaggerated kindness. Only the frequent card games to which Catherine invited her rival revealed the Queen's true feelings. When she was playing cards Anne could not be alone with Henry, and she had to use her deformed right hand. The King could not have failed to notice the little extra nail every time she dealt or took a trick, or that his wife's hands, in contrast, were perfect: small, white and without a blemish. To make sure there were no embarrassing scenes, Henry had housed Anne in a separate wing of the palace, where her rooms were lavishly hung with tapestries.

Catherine was a strong woman, determined not to give in without a struggle. Campeggio, anxious to avoid the question of the divorce, had tried to persuade her to go into a nunnery, where she could live a life of discreet luxury, but the Queen would have none of it. And when Wolsey and Campeggio finally opened their court at Blackfriars in London in May 1529, Catherine saw her chance to get at Henry in public. Throwing herself at his feet, she pleaded for justice, the foreign accent in her voice becoming stronger as emotion took over. 'I take all the world to witness I have been to you a true, humble and obedient wife,' she cried. 'And when ye had me at the first, I take God to be my judge, I was a true maid, without touch of man.' And she swept out of the court, appealing for the case to be heard by the Pope himself in Rome. Henry tried to put a good face on things, summoning aged servants and attendants to give evidence about Catherine and Arthur's wedding night – how the Prince of Wales had been pale and tired in the morning, and how he was heard to say he had been 'in the midst of Spain' during the night. But the public were with Catherine. And then, on the very day that the court was expected to give judgment, Campeggio, acting on instructions from the Pope, adjourned the trial until October.

Henry took refuge in a long summer hunt, moving from palace to mansion in the forests and meadows around London. For Anne, he ordered a sumptuous travelling outfit, with harnesses and horse trappings in black velvet fringed with silk and gold. But although she was equipped like a queen, it was the stout Spanish

Mansell

♟ *The woodcut* above *symbolizes Henry's triumph over Pope Clement, who has fallen from his horse. Bishop John Fisher and Cardinal Reginald Pole attend to the Pope while Henry delivers the Bible to his staunch allies Thomas Cranmer and Thomas Cromwell*

Musée des Beaux Arts, Lille/Giraudon/Bridgeman

♟ *Many people who supported Catherine believed that her nephew Emperor Charles V left would invade England and depose Henry if he divorced her. The invasion never happened, but Charles's pressure on the Pope following his occupation of Rome certainly delayed the court hearing*

woman who still had the title and, as the months dragged on, Anne became increasingly anxious. Always volatile and hot-tempered, she became waspish and imperious, no longer afraid of using her tongue on the King. 'I have been waiting long,' Anne reminded Henry, 'and might in the meanwhile have contracted some advantageous marriage, out of which I might have had issue, which is the greatest consolation in this world; but alas! farewell to my time and youth spent to no purpose'.

A mature beauty

Anne was right; her youth was passing. Now almost 30, she was no longer a slim, enchanting girl but a mature woman, her dark beauty enhanced by the scarlet and crimson gowns the King gave her and the brilliant jewels he ordered for her to wear in her hair. Much as he lusted after Anne and feared to think that she might leave him, Henry gradually began to chafe under her arrogant, unbridled tongue, so different from the dignified words of his wife. In truth, though, Catherine's position was becoming more difficult. She dined with him in public on holy days, but apart from this saw Henry only once every three days. And he no longer treated her as the noble lady whom he loved and respected.

The court did not meet again, and the great Cardinal Wolsey was now a doomed man. The King had expected his chief minister to come up with a divorce and he did not easily forgive those who failed him. Wolsey was dismissed

Stephanoff: The Banquet. Windsor Castle, Royal Library. ©1990 HM the Queen

As negotiations with the Pope dragged on, Henry and Anne abandoned any attempt to keep their love secret and displayed their affection openly in front of the court above. Although Cardinal Wolsey (pictured left) and Anne had reached an uneasy truce – Anne needed the Cardinal's help with the divorce – they always regarded each other with a certain amount of suspicion as they vied for influence over the King. Anne could only have been relieved when her old rival died after a long illness at the end of 1530

from his post as Lord Chancellor and, like Catherine, was charged with putting the Pope's interests above those of the King.

The King then decided to try and force the Pope to give him what he wanted, and saw that this might also be a way to replenish his coffers. In early 1531 he accused the entire English clergy of the crime with which he had charged Wolsey, but agreed to pardon them in return for the monstrously large fine of £100,000. Everyone knew this was a conspiracy, but the clergy paid up and also recognized the King as Supreme Head of the Church of England.

By this time, Henry was constantly in Anne's company and, in the summer of 1531, when she accompanied him on his long summer hunting trip for the first time, they at last became lovers. On the morning the Royal party trotted out of Windsor Castle, Henry left a message for Catherine telling her not to follow him. She never saw her once-loving husband again. While he was away, he sent an order commanding her to leave the castle, and several of her servants were dismissed without warning. Poor Catherine aged ten years overnight. Desperately, she sent Henry a gold cup as a New Year's gift, but he returned it immediately. Henry had made his

decision. He would marry Anne come what may, even if it meant defying the Pope.

On 1 September 1532, in a splendid ceremony at Windsor Castle, the King created his mistress Marquess of Pembroke. Dressed in crimson velvet trimmed with ermine, Anne must have looked at her best, her dark hair flowing free and her black eyes flashing with pride and triumph as the King placed the gold coronet on her head. Soon afterwards, Henry ordered Catherine to send him her jewels so that he could give them to Anne. Catherine was outraged, but she did what she was asked, letting it be known that yet again she had acted as an obedient wife.

Anne's happy news

At the turn of the year, Anne played her final card. She may have begun to suspect she was pregnant during the Christmas festivities, but by the end of January there was no longer any doubt that she was carrying a child, which she hoped would be King Henry's longed-for male heir. The glad news forced Henry's hand. There could be no further delay. Catherine must be divorced and his son born legitimate.

Even by the standards of the day, when

👑During their courtship and in the run-up to their marriage, Henry presented Anne with an extraordinary assortment of gifts. Among them were money, jewels, rich clothing and an exquisite clock. A copy of this clock, which Henry gave to his future Queen in 1532, can be found in Hever Castle *right*

👑As a young member of the court at Malines, Anne learned to play both the lute and clavichord and became an accomplished musician. She sang her own songs and accompanied herself on her elegant lute, which is still intact *right*

👑*Left* A page illustrating *The Annunciation* is part of Anne Boleyn's illuminated book of hours. She was a devoted Catholic who cherished many of the ceremonies of the medieval church – but she also used this volume to exchange love letters with Henry. On this page was inscribed the following couplet: 'Be daly prove you shalle me fynde, to be to you bothe lovyng and kynde'

BRIEF HAPPINESS

ON THE DAY OF HER CORONATION, ANNE WAS TRIUMPHANT. SHE WAS THE KING'S WIFE, SHE WAS EXPECTING HIS HEIR AND SHE WAS NOW QUEEN. BUT HER JOY WAS TO BE SHORT-LIVED

ANNE WAS SO EXCITED BY HER PREGNANCY and so exultant that she and Henry were finally married that she could hardly contain herself. Even in the early months of the year, when she was not supposed to tell anyone about the baby or the secret wedding ceremony, she could not stop herself from dropping huge hints. She informed her uncle, the Duke of Norfolk, that she would go on a pilgrimage immediately after Easter if she was not by then with child. A few days later, when she happened to see Sir Thomas Wyatt, she could not resist virtually telling him what was in the wind. 'Three days ago,' she laughed, 'I had a sudden wild desire to eat apples, which I have never liked. The King says it is a sign that I am pregnant, but I tell him I cannot be.'

Henry was not much better at concealing things than his new Queen, and dropped hints as broad as hers. But after Cranmer's consecration and his ruling on the wedding, there was no longer any need to keep the marriage secret. Queen Catherine was bluntly informed that she was no longer the King's wife and would in future be known as the Princess Dowager.

Lavish preparations

Preparations for Anne's Coronation began immediately and the warm spring days were soon filled with the sort of fuss and attention the new Queen loved. Her first-floor apartment at Greenwich Palace was redecorated and refurnished, and on all the King's palaces and houses masons obliterated Catherine of Aragon's coat of arms and carved that of Anne Boleyn instead. With typical flamboyance Anne chose to have the motto *La plus heureuse* (The most happy) embroidered across the doublets of her

♛ *When Henry married Anne he was no longer either slim or youthful, but his impressive stature and finery created an imposing presence* left. *His new Queen* above *shared a love of rich fabrics and dazzling jewellery which complemented her dark colouring*

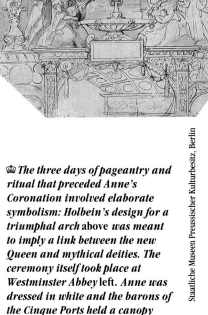

♛ *The three days of pageantry and ritual that preceded Anne's Coronation involved elaborate symbolism: Holbein's design for a triumphal arch* above *was meant to imply a link between the new Queen and mythical deities. The ceremony itself took place at Westminster Abbey* left. *Anne was dressed in white and the barons of the Cinque Ports held a canopy made of cloth-of-gold over her as the procession made its way through the streets*

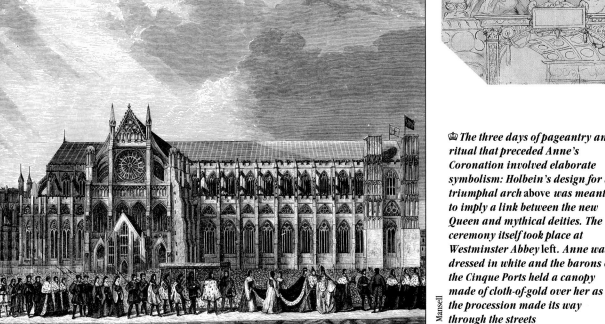

servants' new blue and purple livery.

The magnificent pomp and ceremony accompanying Anne's Coronation lasted four days. On 29 May 1533 Anne, clad in cloth-of-gold, was rowed upriver from Greenwich Palace in the Queen's barge, attended by a flotilla decked out in flags and coloured bunting. The bells of the City churches rang out, and the guns of Henry's warships and the Tower thundered welcome as she arrived. Her Coronation procession through the streets of London two days later was talked about for generations afterwards. Pageants performed on the King's instructions likened Anne to the mother of the Virgin Mary, saluting her nobility, beauty and chastity, although all could see her swollen belly. On Whit Sunday, 1 June, Anne was crowned with great splendour in Westminster Abbey.

An unpopular Queen

After six long years of broken promises, disappointments and delays, Anne's hour of glory had arrived at last. But she cannot have failed to notice that the crowd outside was hostile, or to hear the bawdy insults and the occasional shouts of 'witch' and 'harlot'. It was Catherine whom they loved, not this upstart.

That year, the King did not spend months away from the capital hunting. He passed the summer protectively close to Anne, never venturing far from London. The longest day of the year soon came and then summer began to slide gently into autumn. As Anne entered her

Windsor Castle, Royal Library ©1990 HM the Queen

♛Above *Holbein's intimate sketch of a woman, presumed to be the Queen without her regal trappings, shows her in pensive mood. But beneath her apparently mild demeanour lay a woman with a volatile temperament, who was capable of inspiring both absolute devotion and extreme hatred. Despite the fact that her position was dependent upon the unreliable goodwill of her husband, she found it hard to curb her tongue or play the submissive wife*

♛*Anne had a taste for the theatrical, and enjoyed taking part in private masques and plays. Here she is shown in the costume of St Barbara* left

eighth month of pregnancy, she retired to her chamber, where the August sun and heat were shut out by heavy tapestries.

But now, at the very moment when the time she had longed for had come, Anne was sick at heart. She had heard rumours that Henry had taken another mistress, and when she confronted him the King rounded on her. Did she not know, he shouted, that he could at any time lower her as much as he had raised her?

The new Princess

On Sunday 7 September, between three and four in the afternoon, the Queen gave birth to a daughter. A murmur ran through the waiting court. The customary *Te Deum* was rung from the church steeples, but Henry ordered no public celebrations. No joust was to be held and no bonfires were lit in honour of the new child. But at least Anne had the satisfaction of hearing a herald proclaim her daughter the lawful heiress to the throne in place of the Princess Mary.

The little girl was called Elizabeth. She was given over to the care of a wet nurse the moment the ceremony was over and spirited away to Hatfield House, north of London, where her half-sister Mary was already in residence.

For Henry's elder daughter the new baby was a disaster. Denied all her Royal privileges and forbidden to see her mother, she was now expected to defer to the tiny infant. Proud and defiant, she refused. In punishment, Henry stripped her of her jewels and her fine clothing.

At Christmas Anne was generous. For the King she ordered a miniature gilded fountain in the shape of three naked women inset with rubies, pearls and diamonds; the water gushed from their breasts. But all was not going well with her husband. For years the thrill of the chase and thwarted desire had stoked Henry's passion for Anne to boiling point. Now that he had Anne safely in his pocket, her appeal faded and his ardour cooled. He began to be irritated by his new Queen. The woman he had once found so exciting and intriguing had turned from a vivacious, sensuous girl into a demanding, shrewish woman. Her sharp tongue, and her frenzied rages when she did not get her own way, wearied him. Ousting Catherine had not brought the hoped-for ease and contentment.

Michael Holford

Roy Miles Fine Paintings, London/Bridgeman

👑 *While she was still a very young baby, Elizabeth was given her own establishment at Hatfield House in Hertfordshire* above, *where she was looked after by Anne's aunt, Lady Bryan*

👑 *Anne saw little of her daughter – depicted* left *at the ages of three, five and six – and major decisions about her upbringing were made by the King and Council*

'Henry is bewitched by this cursed woman...does all she says and dares not contradict her'

IMPERIAL AMBASSADOR
CHAPUYS ON ANNE

Ronald Sheridan Ancient Art and Architecture Collection

'I was seduced into this marriage by sorcery, therefore I believe it to be null'

HENRY

♛ *Anne's downfall is enshrined in stained glass: this roundel shows the arms of her rival – Jane Seymour – impaled by those of Henry VIII left*

DISSOLUTION OF THE MONASTERIES

Forcing the clergy to accept him rather than the Pope as their Supreme Head was only the beginning of Henry VIII's attack on the Church. For many years the King had cast covetous eyes on the prosperous estates and valuable possessions of the 800 or so monasteries, nunneries and friaries dotted throughout the country. As his own finances worsened, the idea of seizing their wealth for himself became more and more attractive. Henry's cunning mind also saw that he could get what he wanted while appearing to launch a crusade against lax behaviour and mismanagement: many people thought that monks and nuns led indulgent and immoral lives, and very little of a monastery's income went to help the poor and needy.

The first inspectors sent out in 1535 did not have much difficulty in finding what the King wanted, coming back with tales of homosexuality and of abbots found cloistered with their mistresses. In 1536, Henry made his move, dissolving all the smaller houses with incomes of under £200 a year. This was a very limited operation, which left the really wealthy monasteries untouched, but it helped to trigger off a series of rebellions in October 1536 known as the Pilgrimage of Grace. A second spate of attacks began with the surrender of the great Cluniac priory of Lewes in November 1537. By March 1540 there were no religious houses left anywhere in England or Wales, and an estimated 10,000 monks and nuns had been pensioned off. Many found alternative occupations and several got married.

Financially, the King did not do as well out of the Dissolution as he should have done, as his need for cash led him to sell everything almost as soon as he acquired it

City of Bristol Museum and Art Gallery/Bridgeman

GROWING TENSIONS

By the late summer of 1534, the new Queen was again anxious. The people were hostile, the King still had no male heir and, so it was rumoured, was thinking of other women who might provide one. Two pregnancies earlier in the year had ended in miscarriage, and the symptoms of a third had proved to be a false alarm. Like Catherine, it seemed, Anne could not carry her children to term. When the truth finally dawned on Henry he was furious, and took comfort again in the 'very beautiful damsel' with whom he had solaced himself the previous year.

Throughout the autumn and winter of 1534, Anne saw alarming evidence that Henry was indeed tired of her. The courtiers, sensing which way the wind was blowing, suddenly began to pay their respects once more to Princess Mary, whom they had been shunning ever since her mother's fall. In November, Francis I of France, at whose court Anne had once shone, revived the previously abandoned agreement to marry Princess Mary to his son, the Dauphin; the French envoy who came to discuss the match ignored the unhappy Queen and brought her no customary gift or greetings. The awful possibility must have dawned on Anne: Henry had rid himself of one wife. What was to stop him doing away with a second?

Anne's hopes dashed

The following summer, Henry and Anne set out on the usual annual progress, hunting and hawking their way west through Wiltshire to the borders of Wales. Anne was pregnant again and in high spirits. But the King longed to replace his thin, nagging wife.

Then, almost like a miracle, Henry met a woman who seemed to be everything he wanted. While staying at Wolf Hall in Wiltshire, the house of Sir John Seymour, the King was introduced to his host's 26-year-old daughter Jane, a demure, pale girl with blue-grey eyes.

Soon Anne had to suffer the humiliation of seeing Jane flaunt her youth dressed in the King's silks and velvets, his jewels around her neck. The young woman was well schooled by self-interested courtiers. Taking Anne as their example, they coached Jane on how to conduct herself, telling her she must not 'in any circumstances whatever yield to the King's desire except by right of marriage'. Jane was not as clever or educated as Anne, but she had just enough wit to learn her lesson. Inflamed by her resistance to his advances, Henry was soon besotted with her.

On 7 January 1536, Catherine of Aragon died, her last days spent doubled over with violent stomach pains and vomiting uncontrollably. Many believed she had been poisoned by a substance put into her beer. When he heard the news Henry was overjoyed, and immediately ordered an elaborate funeral in Peterborough Abbey, where Catherine was to be buried as the wife of Prince Arthur.

That same month, Henry took part in a tournament at Greenwich. As luck would have it, he was unhorsed, fell heavily to the ground and was knocked unconscious for two hours. Shocked by the news of Henry's accident, which was broken to her abruptly by her uncle, the Duke of Norfolk, Anne miscarried a son. Making his way to the chamber where she still lay in pain, Henry glowered at her: 'I will speak to you when you are recovered,' he said menacingly, and strode away. The King was now convinced that Anne had bewitched him and that the

Ashmolean Museum, Oxford

Kunsthistorisches Museum, Vienna

passion he had once felt for her was so strong and unnatural only sorcery could have inspired it. He never slept with her again.

Jane, meanwhile, continued to tantalize the King. When Henry sent her a letter and a purse full of gold sovereigns, she kissed the letter but returned it to the messenger unopened saying that she could not accept the gift. Then, throwing herself on her knees, she addressed herself to Henry through his messenger, begging him to remember she was a gentlewoman, born of good and honourable parents, and that if he wished to send her money, she prayed that it might be when God had sent him a good marriage. This well-rehearsed little performance

♕ *Henry began his serious flirtation with Jane Seymour* above *in September 1535, but he may well have noticed her at court before that date. Although she lacked Anne's fiery brilliance, Jane had a gentleness that held a strong attraction for a King weary of constant arguments*

♕ *The King asked Hans Holbein to design a gold cup for Jane. A drawing of it* left *shows that the legend 'Bound to obey' was to be included – an indication of what Henry expected from his consort*

35

 For Anne's uncle, Thomas Howard, third Duke of Norfolk above, *politics came before family sentiment. When the King tired of Anne, Howard stood in judgement at her trial, unmoved by pity or tenderness. Yet he was quick to spot the potential for his own advancement when Henry became attracted to Catherine Howard, another of his nieces*

By gracious permission of HM the Queen

was the final nail in Anne's coffin.

The ultimate blow fell a few weeks later. Informally, by innuendo, a case was built against Anne, and on 24 April the King authorized a commission to investigate charges of treason relating to the Queen and her closest friends. For the sake of appearances, a few days were spent on inquiries; then the accusations began. At the May Day tournament at Greenwich, where Anne was unwise enough to drop a handkerchief to her favourite, the King was informed that his Queen had committed adultery with five men: Mark Smeaton, a favourite musician; Henry Norris, Sir Francis Weston and William Brereton, all of whom were members of the King's most intimate circle; and her own brother, George, Lord Rochford. These trumped-up charges were all based on the game of courtly love which Anne played with such skill and which she had learned as a young girl at the court of Francis I.

Fatal flirtations

The Royal lawyers insisted that the flirtatious exchanges and gallant compliments overheard in her chambers masked passionate affairs and that the five men on whom she sharpened her suggestive repartee and who praised her with such eloquence had also slept with her.

According to her accusers, Anne had told her lovers that the King was almost impotent, and they had plotted together to assassinate him, the idea being that Anne would then marry Norris and rule as Regent for the infant Elizabeth. Smeaton was brought from Greenwich to the Tower that same evening, while the others were arrested and questioned.

Daunted by her forthcoming ordeal, the Queen paused for a moment above *before entering the Tower* far right. *She was to face an agonizing wait before she was found guilty of incest, adultery and high treason, but she retained her pride to the end*

THE AGEING KING

As Henry got older he was increasingly plagued by chronic headaches and by open ulcers on his legs. The first red swelling appeared in 1528, when he was 37, and this painful condition was with him until he died.

Some people believe that Henry's ulcers were syphilitic, but it is far more likely the ulcers were caused by untreated varicose veins, damaged and infected by constant exercise. Another possibility is that they were the result of a jousting injury, which had caused splinters of bone to work their way agonizingly to the surface. The pain of his ulcers was sometimes so great that Henry could hardly walk, and at the end of his life he had to be carried everywhere. The King made matters worse by continuing to eat gargantuan meals even when he was no longer hunting every day, and he rapidly put on weight. In his 50s he was positively gross, with a waist of 54 inches. Not surprisingly, in his later years he was bad-tempered and unpredictable

Mansell

'I heard say the executioner is very good, and I have a little neck'

ANNE

On such a basis was a Queen of England found guilty and condemned to death. Anne awaited her end with composure. Proud to the last, she did not beg Henry for mercy. The men were dispatched on Tower Hill on 17 May. Anne, expecting to be summoned at any moment, found her execution was postponed for 48 hours so she could be divorced before she died, and her daughter Elizabeth declared a bastard.

Pride facing death

At the end, Henry showed some mercy, ordering that Anne should be beheaded on the little green within the Tower, rather than before the silent crowds who had gathered on Tower Hill beyond the walls. He also granted her request that she should die by the sword rather than the axe, and he arranged for an executioner to be brought over from France specially. On the morning of 19 May, dressed in a gown of grey damask lined with fur, Anne walked out in the spring sunshine. Although exhausted and drained, she walked erect, and climbed without faltering up the steps of the newly erected scaffold. Here, she carefully tucked her hair into a plain linen cap and made a short speech, speaking well of the King. She neither admitted nor denied her guilt. Bowing her head, she called on Jesus to receive her spirit and gave the signal to the executioner. There was a flash of light as the sun caught the great, two-handed sword. One of her ladies picked up Anne's head, the others her body, and both were carried into the little chapel of St Peter ad Vincula by the Green, where the Queen was unceremoniously buried. She had gambled everything for Henry, and she had lost.

E M Ward: Anne Boleyn at the Queen's Stairs. Sunderland Museum and Art Gallery/Tyne and Wear Museums

The next day, on a warm spring afternoon, Anne herself was rowed upriver, a crowd of gaping Londoners gathering to see her arrive at the watergate of the Tower. To increase her agony, the Queen was kept in the very room where she had slept on the night before her Coronation.

Trial and punishment

Except for Smeaton, who confessed under torture, all the accused steadfastly maintained their innocence. Nonetheless, they were tried on 12 May by a court which included Anne's uncle, the Duke of Norfolk. They were all found guilty and sentenced to be hung, drawn and quartered.

More sensational was the trial of Anne and her brother which took place in the Tower three days later before Norfolk and 26 other peers. The government's accusations were shameless, and Anne's supposed intimacy with her brother conjured up in salacious detail. In the end, it was said, 'Lord George Rochford...despising every law of human nature...violated and carnally knew... his own natural sister.'

Mansell

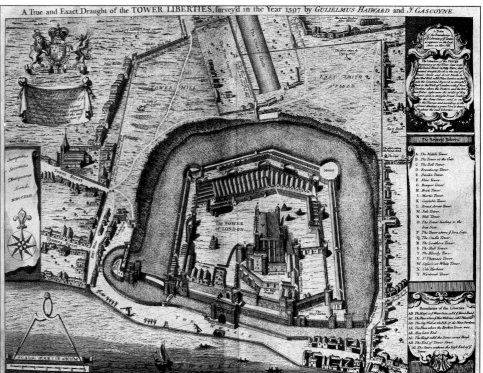

HAMPTON COURT

Originally built by Wolsey at vast expense, Hampton Court and all of its contents were offered to Henry VIII in 1525 in a vain attempt by the Cardinal to stay in favour. Henry greedily accepted and set out on a major plan of extension and redecoration. Although five of Henry's six wives lived at the palace, it is most closely associated with Catherine Howard, whose ghost was, at one time, said to haunt its rooms and corridors

A F Kersting

🏰Hampton Court Palace's Tudor Gothic front *below* was started by Cardinal Wolsey in 1515 and completed by Henry VIII who made everything on a much grander scale. But Henry was interested in more than just the the palace structure itself. He also became involved in the look of the gardens and, because he was a keen hunter, saw to it that the palace grounds were well stocked with game

🏰The famous astronomical clock, designed to tell the hour, day and month, the number of days since the beginning of the year, phases of the moon and time of high water at London Bridge, was made by Nicholas Oursian in 1540. The clock still adorns the the outer wall of the Anne Boleyn Gateway *above*, where the tragic Queen was believed to have lived before marrying Henry

♛Court tennis was in its heyday in the 16th century and Henry VIII was one of the game's outstanding players. So it was no surprise that Henry had a court installed in his new residence at Hampton Court. The court, which is still in use today *right*, was built in 1530, complete with 12 windows covered with wire netting in order to let in light. In addition to this court, Hampton Court Palace had a number of other sports areas, including three open-air tennis courts, three bowling alleys and a tilt yard where tournaments and jousting were held

♛*Below* Despite the fact that the Cardinal's original kitchen was 48 feet long, it was considered inadequate for catering for the Royal household. So a second kitchen was added. Here, and in the adjacent rooms – such as the pantry, wine and beer cellars, bakehouse and larder – a hundred or more retainers worked under the direction of the master-cook to keep the Royal table loaded with a rich profusion of food

By gracious permission of HM the Queen

By gracious permission of HM the Queen

♛The Great Hall *above*, with its fine hammer beam roof and musician's gallery, was Henry VIII's *tour de force*. It took five years to complete, despite the fact that masons and carpenters were working in shifts around the clock. Anne Boleyn's badges and initials can still be seen among the hall's carvings and tracery, although Jane Seymour had taken her place before the work was completely finished

A F Kersting

Michael Holford

National Portrait Gallery, London

👑 *Above* Henry's eldest child Mary, Catherine of Aragon's daughter, succeeded to the throne when Edward died

By gracious permission of HM the Queen

👑Jane Seymour bore Henry his only legitimate son, Edward *above*, who became King at nine and died at 15

👑 *Left* Princess Elizabeth, the daughter of Anne Boleyn, at about 13 years old

👑Henry's illegitimate son Henry Fitzroy, the Duke of Richmond *right*, died aged 17 from tuberculosis. His mother, Bessie Blount, was Henry's mistress during his first marriage

By gracious permission of HM the Queen

THE LION IN WINTER

**AS SOON AS HE COULD, HENRY WED JANE SEYMOUR, WHO BORE HIM
A LONG-AWAITED SON AND HEIR, AND THEN DIED. THREE MORE
WIVES FOLLOWED, BUT ONLY THE LAST PROVED SATISFACTORY**

 HILE ANNE LANGUISHED IN THE TOWER, Henry was jolly, attending a party nearly every night and sometimes revelling into the small hours. He would tell all around him that he believed Anne had been enjoyed by more than a hundred men, and that she surely must have been a witch to ensnare him so. Even some of his most hardened courtiers were shocked by his heartless and callous behaviour.

When Henry heard that Anne had been beheaded, he set off at once to see Jane, dressed in his brightest clothes. Ten days later, on 30

This dynastic portrait of Henry's family below shows the King flanked by his three legitimate children and – possibly – his favourite wife: (from the left) Princess Mary, Prince Edward, Jane Seymour and Princess Elizabeth. The man carrying a monkey on his back is thought to be Will Somers, the King's jester. Parts of Whitehall Palace and Westminster Abbey, and one of the turrets of Henry's tennis court, can be seen through the arches

May, Jane's 'good marriage' took place. The wedding itself was private and there was no coronation but, early in June, Jane was publicly displayed as Henry's Queen when she accompanied him to the State Opening of Parliament. After Anne, the King's quiet and submissive new wife was a blessed relief. And her influence seemed all to the good. Unlike Anne, who had helped to turn the King against his elder daughter, Jane sought to reconcile Henry and Mary. That summer, Henry visited his elder daughter for the first time in five years, and Mary even played games with her baby half-sister.

Eighteen months later, on 12 October 1537, came the crowning blessing of Henry and Jane's union. The new Queen gave birth to a son at Hampton Court. At last Henry had a legitimate male heir. The boy was healthy, but his mother exhausted by the rough surgery which passed for a Tudor Caesarean, died 12 days later, apparently of septicaemia. For the only time in his life, Henry's grief was massive and sincere. He ordered that Jane's body was to lie in state for more than a fortnight in her chamber at Hampton Court while the bishops said Mass in relays and 1200 other masses were sung for her soul in the City of London. On a bleak November day a procession headed by Princess Mary bore the body to Windsor, where, alone of all his wives, Jane was buried with great pomp in St George's Chapel. Her son, born on the eve of St Edward's day, was named after England's Royal saint and baptized with suitable grandeur.

Search for a bride

Now Henry, as well as his daughter Mary, was in the marriage market. There was no shortage of candidates for the position of Queen of England, but not surprisingly the King's marital record rather dampened the enthusiasm of most young ladies. One early favourite was Christina, Duchess of Milan, a 16-year-old widow who was said to speak French with a charming lisp and to be fond of hunting and cards. The German

PARVVLE PATRISSA, PATRIÆ VIRTVTIS ET HÆRES
ESTO, NIHIL MAIVS MAXIMVS ORBIS HABET.
GNATVM VIX POSSVNT COELVM ET NATVRA DEDISSE,
HVIVS QVEM PATRIS, VICTVS HONORET HONOS,
ÆQVATO TANTVM, TANTI TV FACTA PARENTIS,
VOTA HOMINVM, VIX QVO PROGREDIANTVR, HABENT
VINCITO, VICISTI, QVOT REGES PRISCVS ADORAT
ORBIS, NEC TE QVI VINCERE POSSIT, ERIT.

♛ *Henry's longed-for son Edward was painted by Holbein holding a rattle at about two years old* above. *He was an intelligent and precocious child who was given a rigorous education. At six he was engaged to Mary Queen of Scots – who was only seven months old at the time – but this betrothal was repudiated by the Scots. When Edward was nine his father died and he became King Edward VI, though the country was virtually ruled by his ambitious uncle, the Duke of Northumberland. Edward, despite his youth, had strong feelings about the divine right of kings and – as a staunch Protestant – the divine truth of Protestantism. He was a frail boy who reigned for only six years, dying of tuberculosis at the age of 15, immediately after saying a prayer he had written himself. He left his country in a chaotic economic situation, torn by opposing religious factions*

painter Hans Holbein the Younger, who had come to England in the 1520s, was sent across Europe to capture her likeness, but the young woman herself had reservations, demanding guarantees for the safety of her person; and there were political problems as well. Then there was Louise, the beautiful young daughter of the Duke of Guise, who, the French ambassador assured Henry, had the distinct advantage of being a virgin.

An embarrassing moment

Henry suggested that Louise and any other potential French candidates should be shepherded by Francis I to a meeting at Calais, where the ladies could parade before him and he could pick the one he liked most. Even the licentious French king was deeply shocked, saying it was not the custom in his country to treat damsels of good birth like horses being offered for sale and that it would be terribly humiliating for the ladies he did not choose. The French envoy pushed the point home harder: 'Wouldn't you like to go further, sire,' he asked, 'and ride them all, one after the other, and afterward keep the one who was the nicest.' Henry, stung at last, blushed.

When Christina's uncle, the Emperor Charles V, made a truce with Francis, suddenly neither monarch was very keen for a marriage alliance with Henry. Charles even went so far as to state that Henry would have to get a papal dispensation to marry Christina as she was related to Catherine of Aragon. With two such powerful Catholic figures now lined up against him, Henry was in need of Protestant allies.

A German Princess

By the winter he was seeking to marry into the House of Cleves, a duchy on the lower Rhine which had strong connections with the Lutheran princes of Germany. The Princess Anne, he was told, was an outstanding beauty, who surpassed Christina, his earlier choice, 'as the golden sun excelleth the silver moon'. Anne was said to have an equally lovely sister called Amelia, so once again Holbein was sent off to

THE KING'S PAINTER

Henry and his court were immortalized by Hans Holbein the Younger, the talented German painter who settled in England and was taken up by the King. Holbein's portraits show Henry as he really was, an arrogant, bull-like figure, his splayed legs set wide apart as if to support the massive torso and his virility proclaimed in a grotesquely large codpiece, which thrusts out between the skirts of his doublet. The King, who recognized talent when he saw it, kept Holbein busy. As well as portraying Henry and several of his wives, the master painter was also expected to produce murals for rooms in the Royal palaces, and to design jewellery, table silver, weapons, bookbindings, and even Henry's robes. He also worked with the King's goldsmith to produce the magnificent, bed-size cradle ordered for Anne Boleyn's first child which, Henry was sure, would be his longed-for heir

IOANNES HOLPENIVS BA... SILEENSIS
SVI IPSIVS EFFIGIATOR E XLVI

Uffizi, Florence/Scala

paint them both, while the English ambassadors were instructed to send the King full reports on both ladies. By the end of August 1539 Holbein was back, and the Royal fancy lighted on the 24-year-old Anne. The portrait showed a palely pretty girl and the reports, given a rosy glow by optimistic editing, failed to mention she had little education or sense of humour, could not sing or play an instrument and spent most of her time sewing.

Anne of Cleves travelled from Dusseldorf to Calais with a huge retinue and 228 horses, landing at Dover two days after Christmas. The plan was that she would meet the King at Blackheath, just outside London, on 3 January, but Henry could not wait. Improbably disguised, he rushed down to Kent on New Year's Day. There he had a horrible surprise. Although Anne was not unpleasant to look at, she was lumpen and dull, and had no social graces. Returning to London, he greeted her as planned but desperately tried to wriggle out of the marriage, conjuring up legal obstacles which might enable him to escape his 'Flanders mare'. But there was nothing for it and the two were married on 6 January in Henry's chapel at Greenwich. According to Henry, although he slept with Anne every night, or every other night, the marriage was never consummated, and he made not the slightest attempt to cajole her to her wifely duty.

Henry brushed off the failure of his fourth marriage, blaming the loathsomeness of Anne of Cleve's body for his complete lack of sexual desire. That his age might have had some

National Gallery, London

> ## 'I am ashamed that men have so praised her as they have done, and I like her not'
>
> HENRY ON ANNE OF CLEVES

👑 *Christina of Denmark, Duchess of Milan far left, was one of the women Henry considered marrying. The girl, a daughter of the deposed King of Denmark, had married the Duke of Milan at 13 and been widowed within a year. Though Holbein's portrait of her was said to have delighted Henry, negotiations for her hand led to nothing*

Henry could not control his impatience to see Anne of Cleves and dashed down to Rochester in Kent on New Year's Day 1540, laden with presents 'to nourish love', in order to get a glimpse of her. A Victorian artist records him drawing back in distaste but has altered the story slightly – in the print right *Henry is not in disguise as he actually was, but is hidden in a doorway. Holbein is often blamed for Henry's marriage, as he is supposed to have flattered the girl in his portrait* below, *and so encouraged the King to think she was pretty. In fact, though, Holbein probably produced a good likeness, and it was the verbal and written descriptions of the lumpish Anne which misled the King*

bearing on the matter does not seem to have crossed his mind, although he was now nearly 50 and had a waist measurement which matched his years in inches. He was also very far from being as fit as he used to be. As if to prove himself, Henry was soon falling in love with a sensual, provocative girl of 19. Catherine Howard, like Anne Boleyn, was a niece of the Duke of Norfolk, but whereas Anne as a girl had guarded her virginity fiercely, Catherine had long since given hers away. Her relatives vouched for her 'pure and honest condition', but the truth was that Catherine was a practised tart. Brought up by the old Dowager Duchess of Norfolk, her step-grandmother, she had been left very much to do as the fancy took her. And the fancy took her pretty often. First there was her music teacher, with whom she passed many a long afternoon behind the altar of the family chapel. Then came a gentleman of the household called Francis Dereham, and after him her dashing cousin Thomas Culpeper.

Bewitched again

Henry, of course, knew nothing of this. He was once again totally ensnared. The petite, vivacious Catherine became his mistress almost immediately, and in July 1540, in the same month that he divorced Anne of Cleves, the couple were married privately. Just over a week later, when she dined under a cloth of State at Hampton Court, Catherine was publicly acknowledged as Queen. The King seemed a new man, refreshed and rejuvenated, and the court was plunged into a hedonistic summer of parties, jousts and feasting. Meanwhile Anne, remarkably compliant with anything the King suggested, had retired quietly to the country, where she lived happily until her death in 1557 at the age of 42. She probably thought she had got off lightly.

45

THE KING BETRAYED

Anyone who marries for the fifth time does so out of hope rather than experience. But for Henry the blow, when it came, seemed particularly cruel. For Catherine soon resumed business as usual, completely undaunted by the risks she was taking. Two of her former lovers, Dereham and the musician Manox, were appointed members of her household, while a third, Culpeper, was a gentleman of Henry's

Though Henry was by now visibly ageing, he was still an imposing figure below, and recovered much of his former zest for life when he married the young Catherine Howard, his 'rose without a thorn'. No fully authentic likenesses of her survive, but the miniature right may have been painted after her portrait by Holbein. After her death, Henry wed for the last time; his final choice was a mature widow, Catherine Parr below right, the daughter of a Northamptonshire knight

Belvoir Castle/Bridgeman

privy chamber. In the summer of 1541, when Henry embarked on a Royal progress to the north, both his Queen and Culpeper were of the party. Aided and abetted by Lady Rochford, the widow of Anne Boleyn's brother, who really should have known better, Catherine met Culpeper regularly, cuckolding the King even as he was cheered by his northern subjects. The Queen herself would 'in every house seek for the backdoors and backstairs herself'; once, if the evidence against her is to be believed, they even met in her privy. The problem was that winter had married spring. Henry probably simply could not satisfy Catherine's sexual appetites, while his vast bulk and ulcerous legs can hardly have excited her.

Abandoned to her fate

The promiscuous Catherine was doing what Anne Boleyn was supposed to have done. And it was not long before she was found out. On 1 November, the day after the court returned to Hampton Court, the King offered up prayers for 'the good life he led and trusted to lead' with Catherine. At Mass the next day he was handed a piece of paper which contained full details of the Queen's affairs. At first, Henry simply refused to believe what he was told, and then, when he could hide from the truth no longer, dissolved into tears. For a moment his courtiers saw the tired old man behind the regal mask. Manox confessed that he 'had commonly used to feel the secrets and other parts of the Queen's body', Dereham that 'he had known her carnally many times, both in his doublet and hose between the sheets and in naked bed', while Lady Rochford condemned both herself and Culpeper. Catherine was sent upriver as a prisoner to Syon House. Her uncle the Duke of Norfolk, who had so assiduously promoted his niece, now abandoned her to her fate, as he had

NONSUCH PALACE – AN EXTRAVAGANT DREAM

In the last decade of his life, Henry began to build a fairytale palace near Hampton Court. It was like nothing else England had seen, a fantasy of turrets and battlements, towers and cupolas, its façades encrusted with decorative slate and stucco, flags flying from every pinnacle like a ship in full sail. An entire village was destroyed to clear the site, and hundreds of specialist workmen imported from France, Europe and the Low Countries. Six clockmakers toiled to erect a magnificent instrument which overlooked the huge forecourt, and a whole regiment of gardeners laid out the remarkable gardens and planted the 200 pear trees which Henry had had shipped across the Channel. There were statues everywhere and trick fountains. Beyond was a huge park where Henry planned to hunt deer and boar, with a banqueting house hidden among the trees. It was called Nonsuch for there was nothing like it, and it was hideously expensive. Henry died before it was completed, and nothing remains

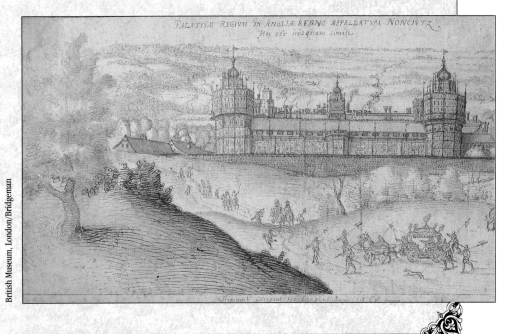

British Museum, London/Bridgeman

National Portrait Gallery, London

once turned against Anne Boleyn.

On 1 December, Culpeper and Dereham were tried at the Guildhall in London on a charge of high treason and were sentenced to be hung, drawn and quartered. Culpeper's sentence was commuted to beheading, but Dereham, even though he was less guilty, had to suffer the full penalty. The two men went to their graves on 10 December, and Catherine and Lady Rochford were executed on Tower Green a few months later, on 13 February 1542. Like Anne, Catherine put up a brave show, although she was not yet 21. When the moment came, while the grey-haired Lady Rochford died in a frenzy, the young girl mounted the scaffold with dignity. She had learned to behave like a queen at last.

His final choice

After a few weeks Henry threw off his grief, and the supper parties and banquets began again. In July 1543, to everyone's surprise, he married again. The King, now so bloated that he was able to walk only with the aid of a stick, was 52. His 31-year-old bride, Catherine Parr, had been married twice before. She was not beautiful but, unlike Henry's previous consorts, she was a wise and responsible woman. Like Anne Boleyn, she was well educated. While Henry became ever more absorbed, plagued by frequent headaches and in constant pain from his ulcered legs, Catherine proved a steady and agreeable companion, who devoted herself to soothing his declining years.

Only once was there a hiccup in their relationship and this was soon smoothed over.

The Queen was an ardent Protestant and she was not afraid to try to convert the King who, to her way of thinking, still clung to the ancient Roman Catholic rituals despite his break with the Pope. Rather unwisely, she let her apartments be used by hot-headed courtiers who were questioning rites which the King still held dear. When her enemies launched a direct attack, Catherine threw herself on the King's mercy, saying she had only argued with him so that she could listen to his learned arguments. Henry beamed. 'And is it even so, sweetheart?' he said, delighted by her humbleness. 'Then perfect friends we are now again.' When one of the Privy Council arrived with a detachment of the guard to arrest Catherine, they found her walking in the garden of Whitehall Palace with Henry, who took the official aside and upbraided him roundly.

Death of a King

By 1546, even walking in the garden was almost too much for Henry. Now virtually immobile, he would be carried about in a chair or litter and winched up and down stairs. On some days he was too ill to get out of bed. It was clear to all around him that he was dying. Catherine was sent off to direct the Christmas festivities at Greenwich, but Henry stayed at Whitehall Palace. A few days after Christmas he made his will, bequeathing the crown to Prince Edward and his heirs and, failing them, to Mary and then to Elizabeth. On the evening of 27 January 1547, the King's physicians realized the end was very near. Archbishop Cranmer was sent for but he made such slow progress on the icy roads that Henry was past speech by the time he arrived. All Henry could do was clutch Cranmer's hand while the priest spoke to him reassuringly of salvation in Christ. The King died at 2.00 am. He was 55 years old and had been on the throne for almost 38 years. As he had asked in his will, he was buried beside Jane Seymour in St George's Chapel at Windsor.

🖾 Above *Henry surrounded by his six wives, starting with Catherine of Aragon at the bottom and going counterclockwise. His sixth wife, Catherine Parr (bottom left), seems to have given the King's children some kind of family life at last. After his death she wed her former suitor, Jane Seymour's brother Thomas, with whom she had fallen in love four years previously. Only a year later, in September 1548, she died at the Seymour manor, Sudeley Castle in Gloucestershire, a week after giving birth to a baby girl*

'Yet is the mercy of Christ able to pardon me all my sins, though they were greater than they be'

HENRY ON HIS DEATHBED